Olivia

Story Starters

Grades 1-3

Written by Veneda Murtha
Illustrated by S&S Learning Materials

ISBN 1-55035-777-8
Copyright 2005
Revised January 2007
All Rights Reserved * Printed in Canada

Published in the United States by:
On The Mark Press
3909 Witmer Road PMB 175
Niagara Falls, New York
14305
www.onthemarkpress.com

Published in Canada by:
S&S Learning Materials
15 Dairy Avenue
Napanee, Ontario
K7R 1M4
www.sslearning.com

At  Glance™

Table of Contents

Introduction

Why Use this Resource

Congratulations on your purchase of a worthwhile classroom resource! This collection of 58 engaging and detailed illustrations will inspire students' creative writing. Images of varying complexities are included so that students with a wide range of critical thinking and writing abilities may engage meaningfully with them. The illustrations may be used as "starters" for a variety of forms of writing, and can be used to augment any writing program. Or, use them as a meaningful "filler" activity when students have extra classroom time.

Organization of the Book

This resource is divided into four sections based on the primary theme of the illustrations:

1. General Fiction
2. Adventure
3. Fantasy
4. Animal Stories

For easy reference, the story genre and illustration number are listed at the bottom of each page.

Each story starter worksheet includes an illustration and corresponding word list, a blank line for the story's title, and numbered blank lines for the story itself. The word list includes key words related to the illustration to help the students begin to think about their overall impression of the image. They should read the word list before writing to stimulate their creative thinking, and you may wish to have them include the list words in their story. The blank lines are numbered so that you may easily give students instructions on how long their creative writing piece should be.

A blank lined page is included at the back of this book (page 64) and may be used to write a story outline, or to continue writing the story itself if the student needs extra space.

Students may be given the Writing Checklist (page 5) after writing a story. The checklist is a useful guide to help them edit and proofread their stories.

How to Use the Illustrations

The story starters may be used as springboards for a variety of forms of creative writing. The most straightforward use is for a simple narrative or short story. Students who would benefit from other writing challenges may enjoy using the story starters to write any of the following:

- Poetry
- A letter to a character
- Diary or journal entry
- Expressing a point of view
- Expressing feelings
- Telling what happened before
- Predicting what may happen next
- And many other forms of writing!

Name: _____ **Story Title:** _____

Writing Checklist

Read your story. Then read each **sentence** below. Circle Yes or No.

		🙂	🙁
1.	My story has a beginning, middle and an end.	Yes	No
2.	I read my story to be sure that it makes sense.	Yes	No
3.	I used lots of interesting details.	Yes	No
4.	Each sentence begins with a capital letter.	Yes	No
5.	Each sentence ends with a punctuation mark (. ? !).	Yes	No
6.	My sentences are complete.	Yes	No
7.	My handwriting is neat.	Yes	No
8.	There are spaces between the words.	Yes	No
9.	I underlined spellings that I wasn't sure about.	Yes	No
10.	I tried to correct the spellings on my own.	Yes	No

Name: _____

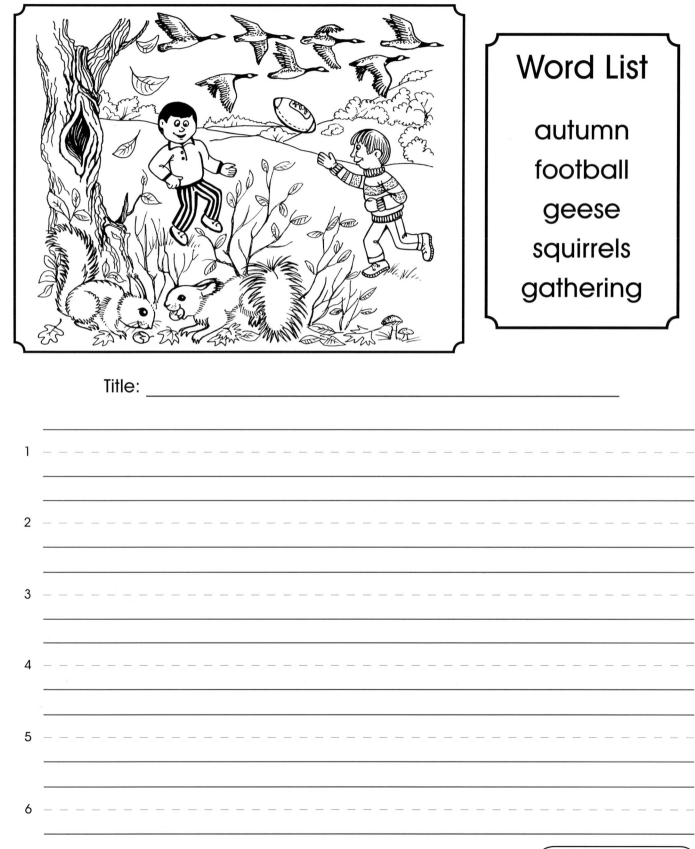

Word List

autumn
football
geese
squirrels
gathering

Title: _____

1 _____

_____

2 _____

_____

3 _____

_____

4 _____

_____

5 _____

_____

6 _____

_____

General Fiction - Illustration 1

Name: _____

Word List

garden

dig

tree

plant

grow

Title: _____

1 _____
_____

2 _____
_____

3 _____
_____

4 _____
_____

5 _____
_____

6 _____
_____

General Fiction - Illustration 2

Name: _____

Word List

post card

letter carrier

deliver

mailbox

read

Title: _____

1 _____

2 _____

3 _____

4 _____

5 _____

6 _____

General Fiction - Illustration 3

Name: _____

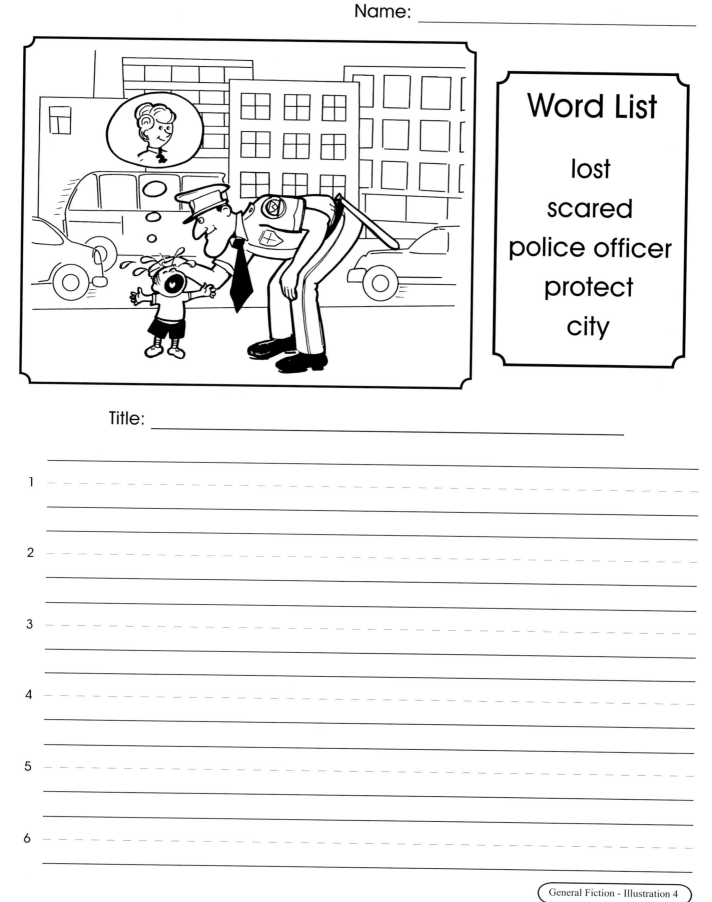

Word List

lost
scared
police officer
protect
city

Title: _____

1 _____
_____

2 _____
_____

3 _____
_____

4 _____
_____

5 _____
_____

6 _____
_____

General Fiction - Illustration 4

Name: _____

Word List

turtle

upset

family

spoon

eat

Title: _____

1 _____

2 _____

3 _____

4 _____

5 _____

6 _____

General Fiction - Illustration 5

Name: _____

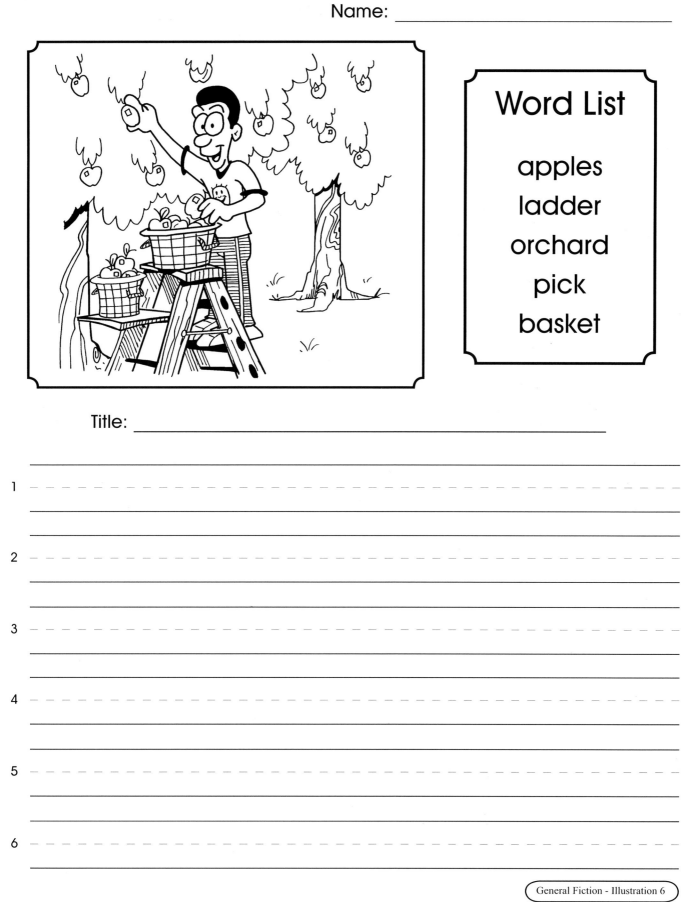

Word List

apples

ladder

orchard

pick

basket

Title: _____

1 _____

2 _____

3 _____

4 _____

5 _____

6 _____

General Fiction - Illustration 6

Name: _____

Word List

classroom

desk

daydream

write

note

Title: _____

1 _____

2 _____

3 _____

4 _____

5 _____

6 _____

General Fiction - Illustration 7

Name: _____

Word List

messy

mad

bedroom

floor

spill

Title: _____

1 --

2 --

3 --

4 --

5 --

6 --

General Fiction - Illustration 8

Name: _____

Word List

paint

easel

draw

colorful

markers

Title: _____

1 _____

2 _____

3 _____

4 _____

5 _____

6 _____

General Fiction - Illustration 9

Name: _____

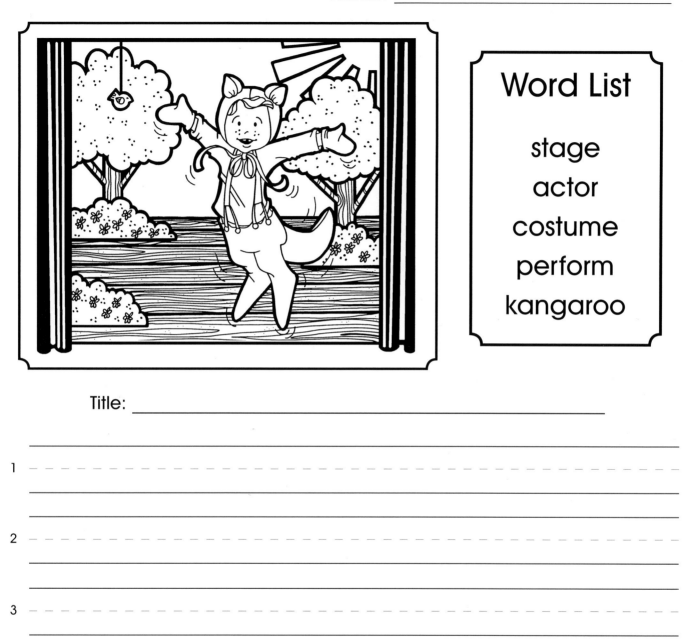

Word List

stage
actor
costume
perform
kangaroo

Title: _____

1 _____

2 _____

3 _____

4 _____

5 _____

6 _____

General Fiction - Illustration 10

Name: _____

Word List

hockey

goal

ice rink

team

skate

Title: _____

1 _____

2 _____

3 _____

4 _____

5 _____

6 _____

General Fiction - Illustration 11

Name: _____

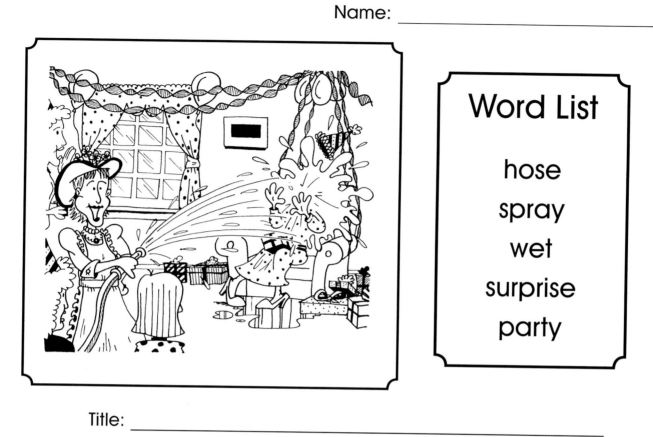

Word List

hose

spray

wet

surprise

party

Title: _____

1 --

2 --

3 --

4 --

5 --

6 --

General Fiction - Illustration 12

Name: _____

Word List

toboggan

snow

slide

steep

hill

Title: _____

1 _____

_____

2 _____

_____

3 _____

_____

4 _____

_____

5 _____

_____

6 _____

_____

General Fiction - Illustration 13

Name: _____

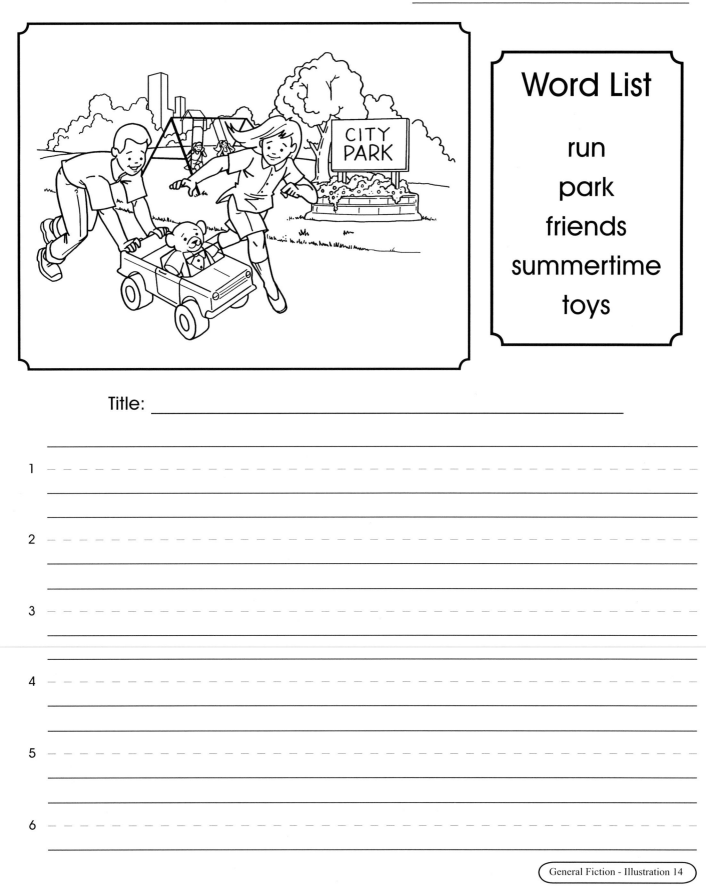

Word List

run

park

friends

summertime

toys

Title: _____

1 _____
   _____

2 _____
   _____

3 _____
   _____

4 _____
   _____

5 _____
   _____

6 _____
   _____

General Fiction - Illustration 14

Name: _____

Word List

dress up

costume

queen

pirate

imagine

Title: _____

1 _____

2 _____

3 _____

4 _____

5 _____

6 _____

General Fiction - Illustration 15

Name: _____

Word List

well

toss

penny

wish

true

Title: _____

1 _____

_____

2 _____

_____

3 _____

_____

4 _____

_____

5 _____

_____

6 _____

_____

General Fiction - Illustration 16

Name: _____

Word List

kite

sky

windy

fly

run

Title: _____

1 _____

2 _____

3 _____

4 _____

5 _____

6 _____

General Fiction - Illustration 17

Name: _____

Word List

trash

pond

collect

help

clean

Title: _____

1 _____

2 _____

3 _____

4 _____

5 _____

6 _____

General Fiction - Illustration 18

Name: _____

Word List

beach

sand

castle

build

sunny

Title: _____

1 _____

2 _____

3 _____

4 _____

5 _____

6 _____

General Fiction - Illustration 19

Name: _____

Word List

nighttime

dark

fire

wood

stars

Title: _____

1 _____

_____

2 _____

_____

3 _____

_____

4 _____

_____

5 _____

_____

6 _____

_____

General Fiction - Illustration 20

Name: _____

Word List

picnic

lunch

fruit

shade

hungry

Title: _____

1 _____

_____

2 _____

_____

3 _____

_____

4 _____

_____

5 _____

_____

6 _____

_____

General Fiction - Illustration 21

Name: _____

Word List

farmer

barn yard

hay

tractor

cows

Title: _____

1 _____

2 _____

3 _____

4 _____

5 _____

6 _____

General Fiction - Illustration 22

Name: _____

Word List

boat

sad

wave

lake

cry

Title: _____

1 _____

_____

2 _____

_____

3 _____

_____

4 _____

_____

5 _____

_____

6 _____

_____

General Fiction - Illustration 23

Name: _____

Word List

cabin

cards

game

club

boys

Title: _____

1 _____

_____

2 _____

_____

3 _____

_____

4 _____

_____

5 _____

_____

6 _____

_____

General Fiction - Illustration 24

Name: _____

Word List

worm
swallow
wiggle
slippery
taste

Title: _____

1 _____

2 _____

3 _____

4 _____

5 _____

6 _____

General Fiction - Illustration 25

Name: _____

Word List

skip

children

grass

exercise

play

Title: _____

1 _____

2 _____

3 _____

4 _____

5 _____

6 _____

General Fiction - Illustration 26

Name: _____

Word List

dive

sea

fish

clam

mask

Title: _____

1 _____

_____

2 _____

_____

3 _____

_____

4 _____

_____

5 _____

_____

6 _____

_____

Adventure - Illustration 27

Name: _____

Word List

chase
ground
dog
sisters
fun

Title: _____

1 _____

2 _____

3 _____

4 _____

5 _____

6 _____

Adventure - Illustration 28

Name: _____

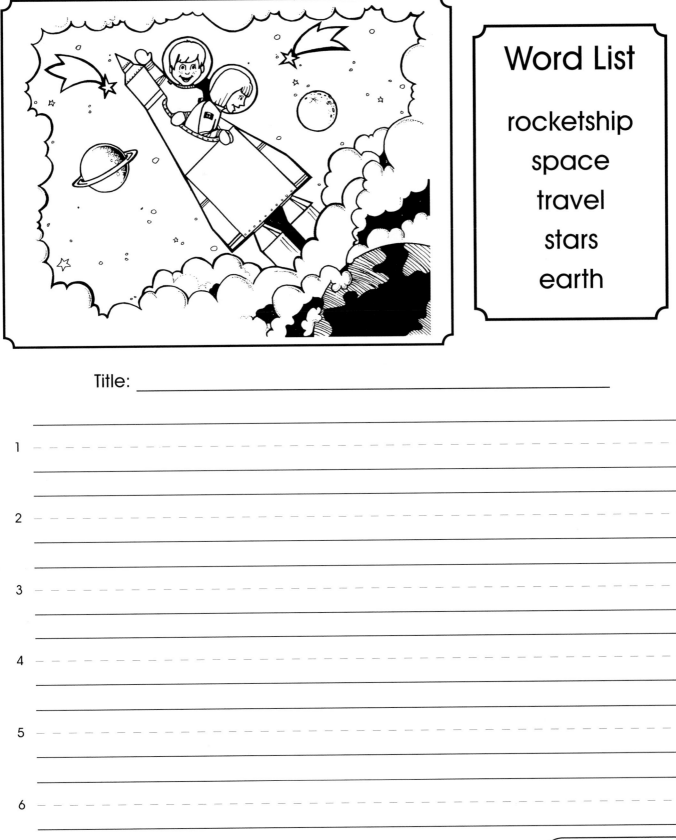

Word List

rocketship
space
travel
stars
earth

Title: _____

1 _____
_____

2 _____
_____

3 _____
_____

4 _____
_____

5 _____
_____

6 _____
_____

Adventure - Illustration 29

Name: _____

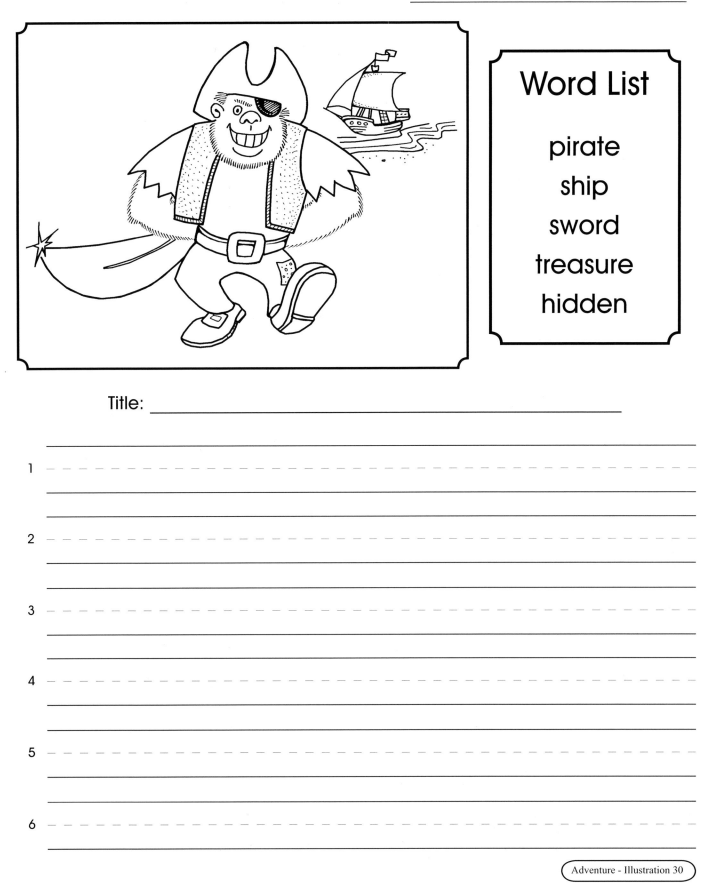

Word List

pirate

ship

sword

treasure

hidden

Title: _____

1 _____

_____

2 _____

_____

3 _____

_____

4 _____

_____

5 _____

_____

6 _____

_____

Adventure - Illustration 30

Name: _____

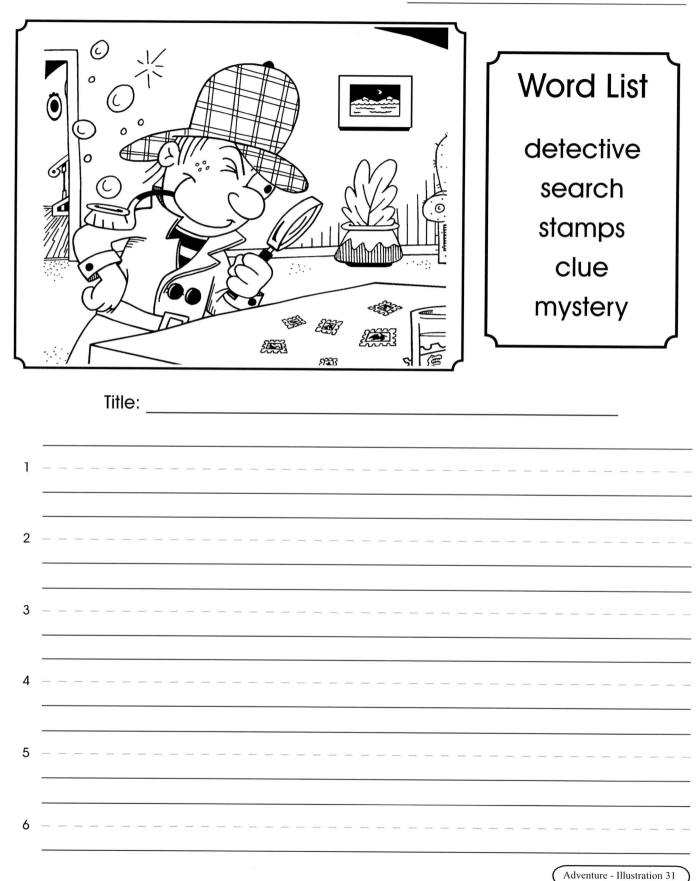

Word List

detective

search

stamps

clue

mystery

Title: _____

1 _____
_____

2 _____
_____

3 _____
_____

4 _____
_____

5 _____
_____

6 _____
_____

Adventure - Illustration 31

Name: _____

Word List

money

bank

thief

escape

steal

Title: _____

1 _____

_____

2 _____

_____

3 _____

_____

4 _____

_____

5 _____

_____

6 _____

_____

Adventure - Illustration 32

Name: _____

Word List

clown
balloon
rides
park
rollercoaster

Title: _____

1 _____

2 _____

3 _____

4 _____

5 _____

6 _____

Adventure - Illustration 33

Name: _____

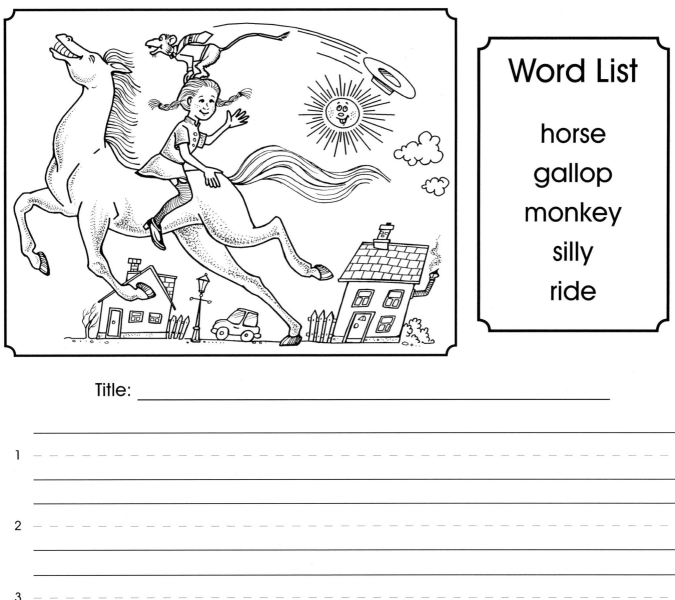

Word List

horse
gallop
monkey
silly
ride

Title: _____

1 _____

_____

2 _____

_____

3 _____

_____

4 _____

_____

5 _____

_____

6 _____

_____

Adventure - Illustration 34

Name: _____

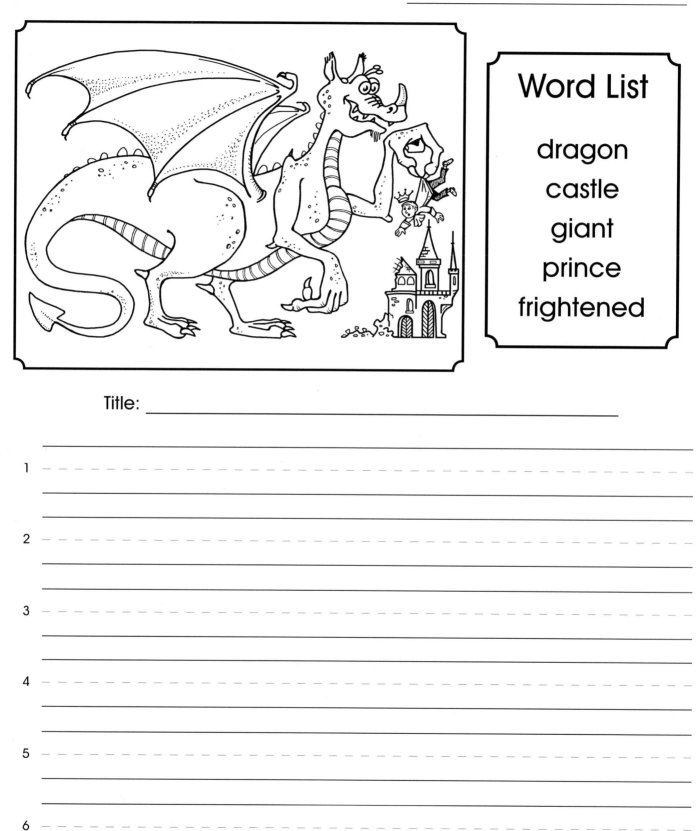

Word List

dragon
castle
giant
prince
frightened

Title: _____

1 _____

2 _____

3 _____

4 _____

5 _____

6 _____

Fantasy - Illustration 35

Name: _____

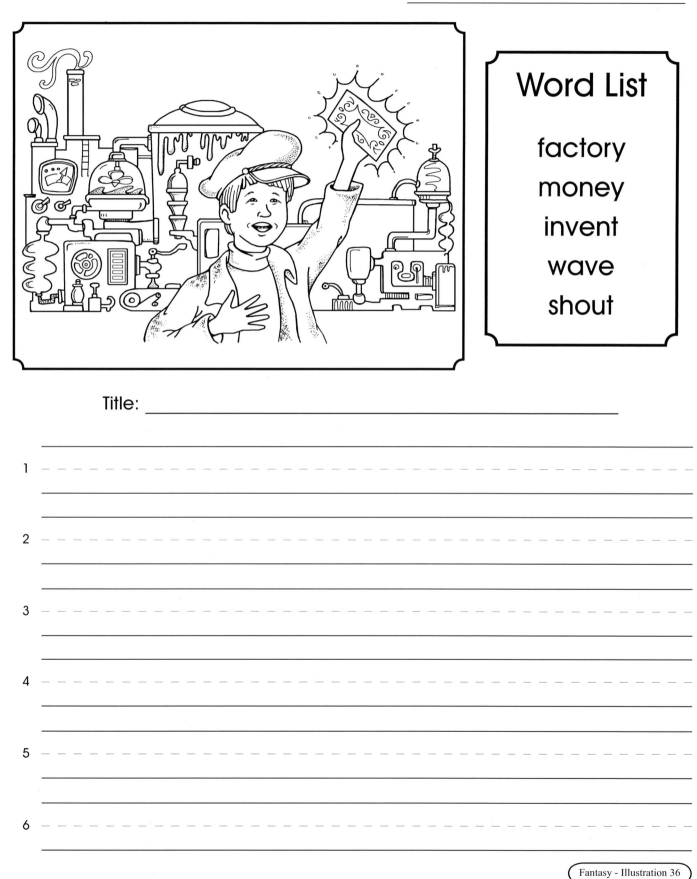

Word List

factory
money
invent
wave
shout

Title: _____

1 _____

2 _____

3 _____

4 _____

5 _____

6 _____

Fantasy - Illustration 36

Name: _____

Word List
giant
supper
little
friendly
waiter

Title: _____

1 _____

_____

2 _____

_____

3 _____

_____

4 _____

_____

5 _____

_____

6 _____

_____

Fantasy - Illustration 37

Name: Olivia Gerwell

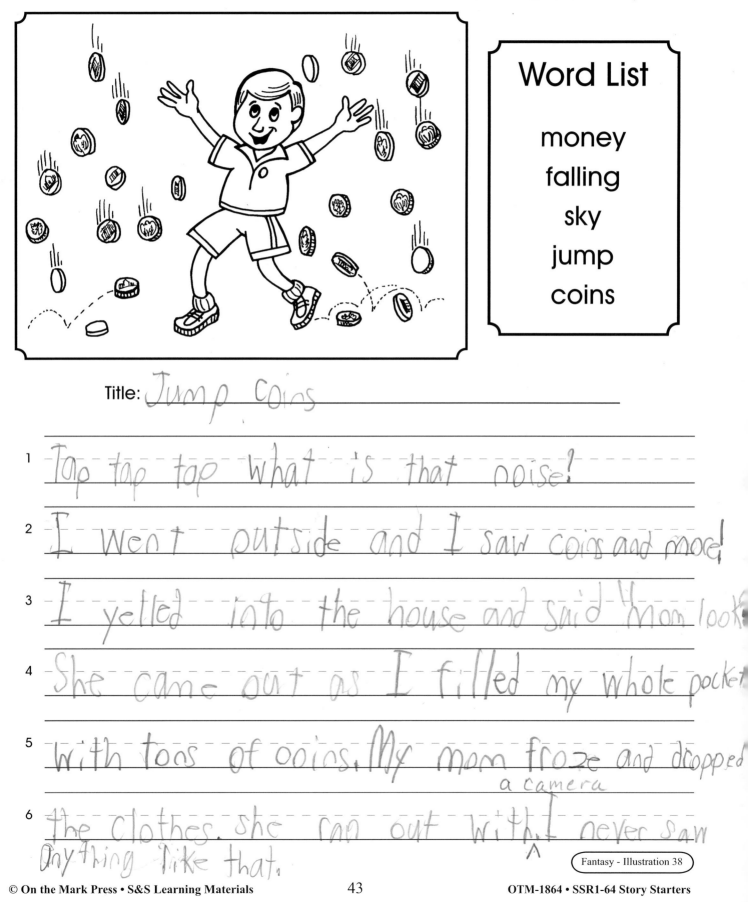

Word List

money
falling
sky
jump
coins

Title: Jump Coins

1 Tap tap tap what is that noise!

2 I went outside and I saw coins and more!

3 I yelled into the house and said "Mom look"

4 She came out as I filled my whole pocket

5 with tons of coins. My mom froze and dropped
   a camera

6 the clothes. she ran out with. I never saw
   anything like that.

Fantasy - Illustration 38

Name: _____

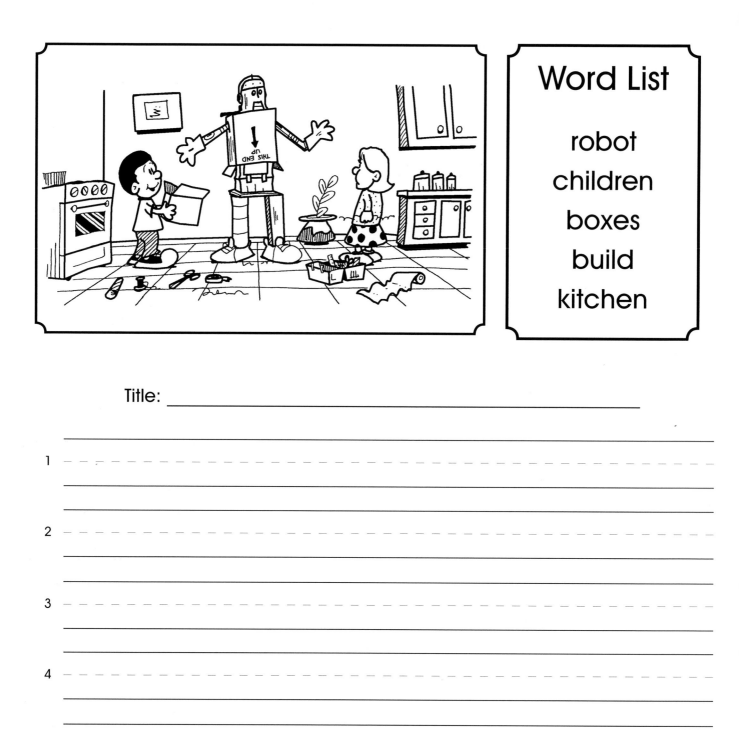

Word List

robot

children

boxes

build

kitchen

Title: _____

1 _____

_____

2 _____

_____

3 _____

_____

4 _____

_____

5 _____

_____

6 _____

_____

Fantasy - Illustration 39

Name: _____

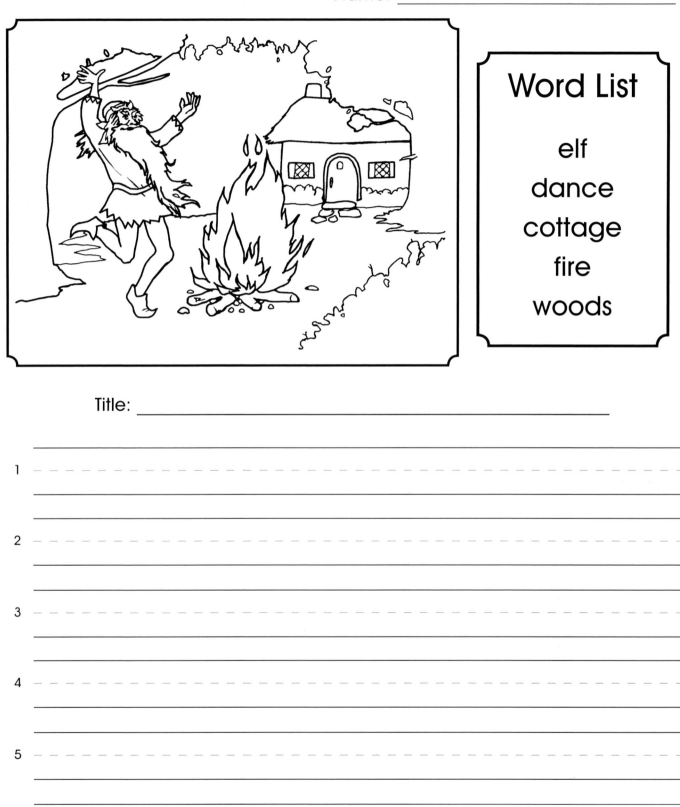

Word List

elf

dance

cottage

fire

woods

Title: _____

1 _____

_____

2 _____

_____

3 _____

_____

4 _____

_____

5 _____

_____

6 _____

Fantasy - Illustration 40

Name: _____

Word List

gold
coins
count
giant
greedy

Title: _____

1 _____
_____

2 _____
_____

3 _____
_____

4 _____
_____

5 _____
_____

6 _____
_____

Fantasy - Illustration 41

Name: _____

Word List

king

fairy

magic

worry

throne

Title: _____

1 _____

_____

2 _____

_____

3 _____

_____

4 _____

_____

5 _____

_____

6 _____

Fantasy - Illustration 42

Name: _____

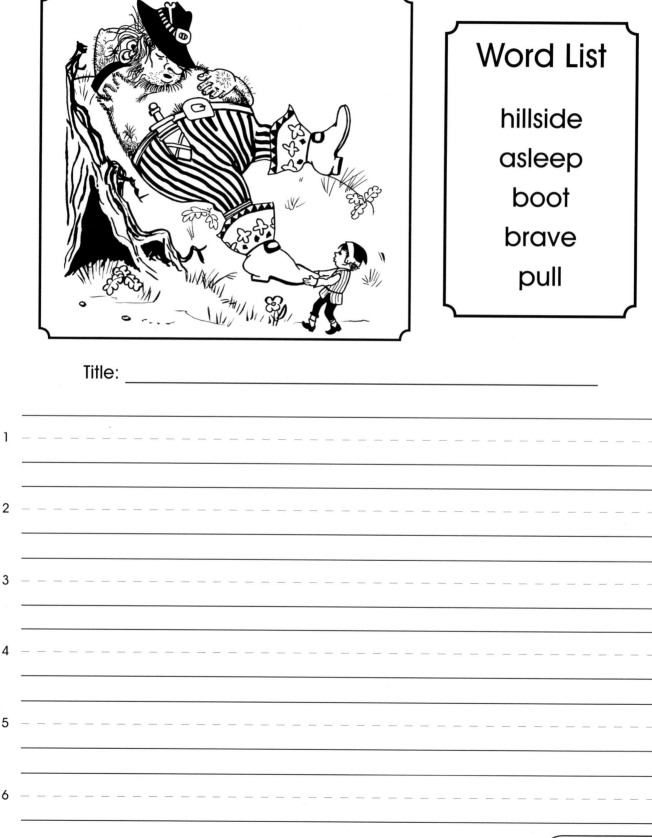

Word List

hillside
asleep
boot
brave
pull

Title: _____

1 _____

2 _____

3 _____

4 _____

5 _____

6 _____

Fantasy - Illustration 43

Name: _____

Word List

school bus
dinosaurs
travel
explore
magic

Title: _____

1 _____

_____

2 _____

_____

3 _____

_____

4 _____

_____

5 _____

_____

6 _____

_____

Fantasy - Illustration 44

Name: _____

Word List

fountain

water

chocolate

messy

surprise

Title: _____

1 _____

_____

2 _____

_____

3 _____

_____

4 _____

_____

5 _____

_____

6 _____

_____

Fantasy - Illustration 45

Name: _____

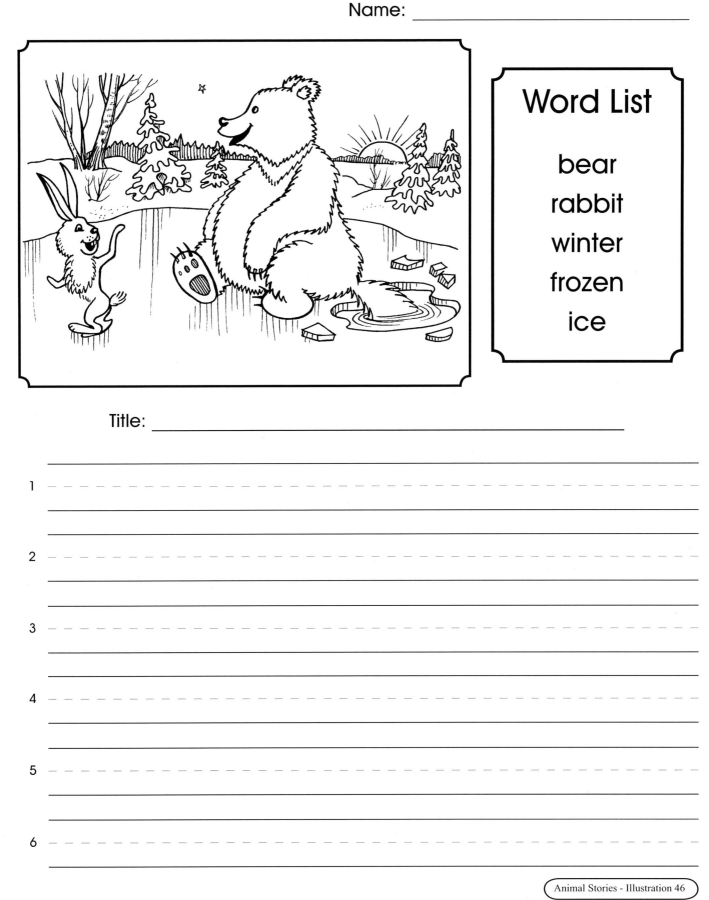

Word List

bear
rabbit
winter
frozen
ice

Title: _____

1 _____

_____

2 _____

_____

3 _____

_____

4 _____

_____

5 _____

_____

6 _____

_____

Animal Stories - Illustration 46

Name: _____

Word List
garbage
cat
mouse
full
sleepy

Title: _____

1 _____

_____

2 _____

_____

3 _____

_____

4 _____

_____

5 _____

_____

6 _____

_____

Animal Stories - Illustration 47

Name: _____

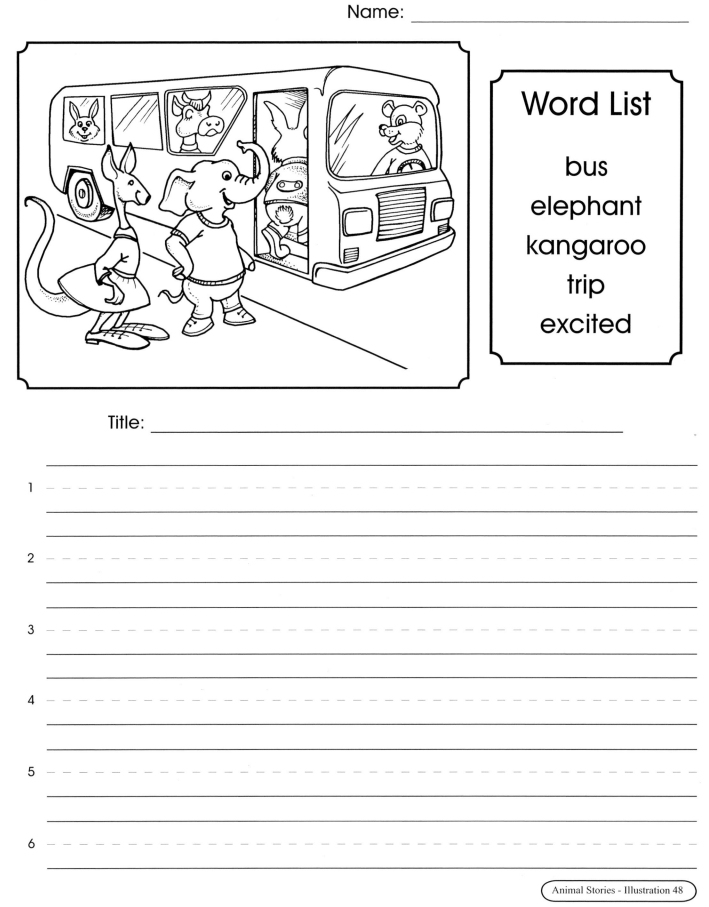

Word List

bus

elephant

kangaroo

trip

excited

Title: _____

_____

1 _____

_____

2 _____

_____

3 _____

_____

4 _____

_____

5 _____

_____

6 _____

_____

Animal Stories - Illustration 48

Name: _____

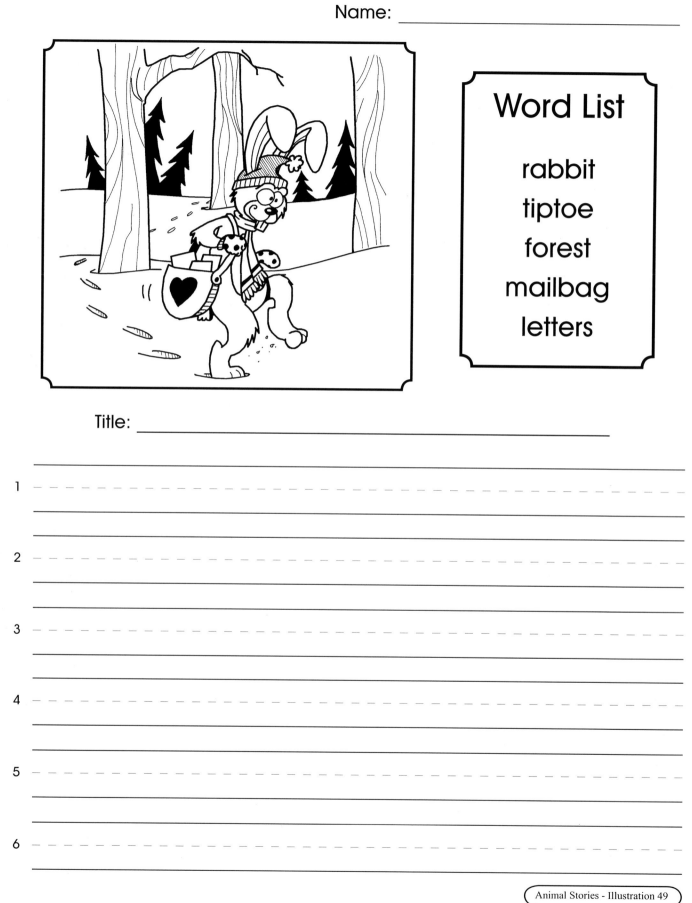

Word List

rabbit

tiptoe

forest

mailbag

letters

Title: _____

1 ─────────────────────────────
_____
_____

2 ─────────────────────────────
_____
_____

3 ─────────────────────────────
_____
_____

4 ─────────────────────────────
_____
_____

5 ─────────────────────────────
_____
_____

6 ─────────────────────────────
_____

Animal Stories - Illustration 49

Name: _____

Word List

bear

hungry

gopher

hide

enemy

Title: _____

1 _____
_____

2 _____
_____

3 _____
_____

4 _____
_____

5 _____
_____

6 _____

Animal Stories - Illustration 50

Name: _____

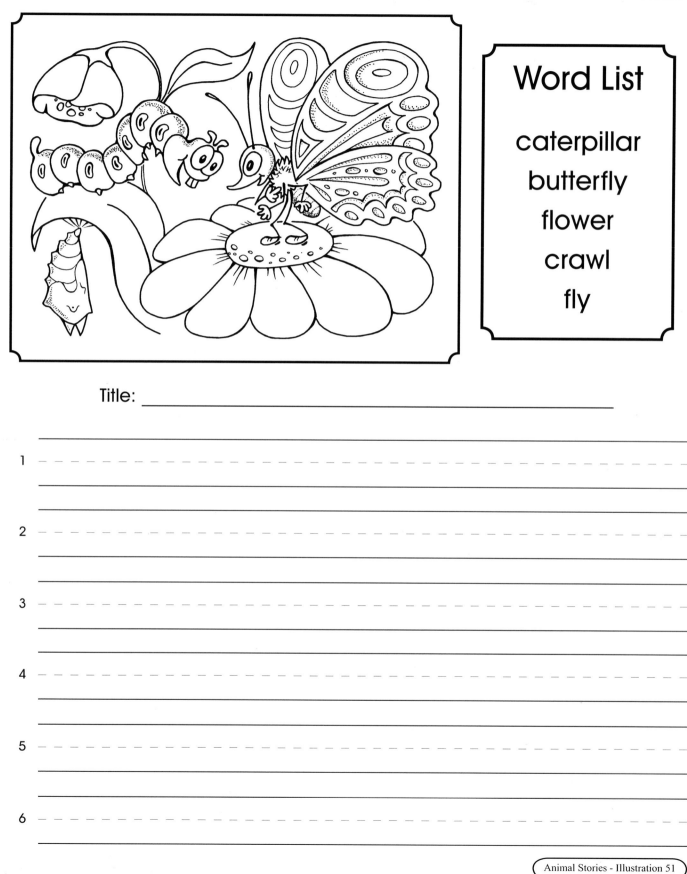

Word List

caterpillar
butterfly
flower
crawl
fly

Title: _____

_____

1 _____

_____

2 _____

_____

3 _____

_____

4 _____

_____

5 _____

_____

6 _____

_____

Animal Stories - Illustration 51

Name: _____

Word List

mouse
street
car
danger
chase

Title: _____

_____

1 -

_____

2 -

_____

3 -

_____

4 -

_____

5 -

_____

6 -

_____

Animal Stories - Illustration 52

Name: _____

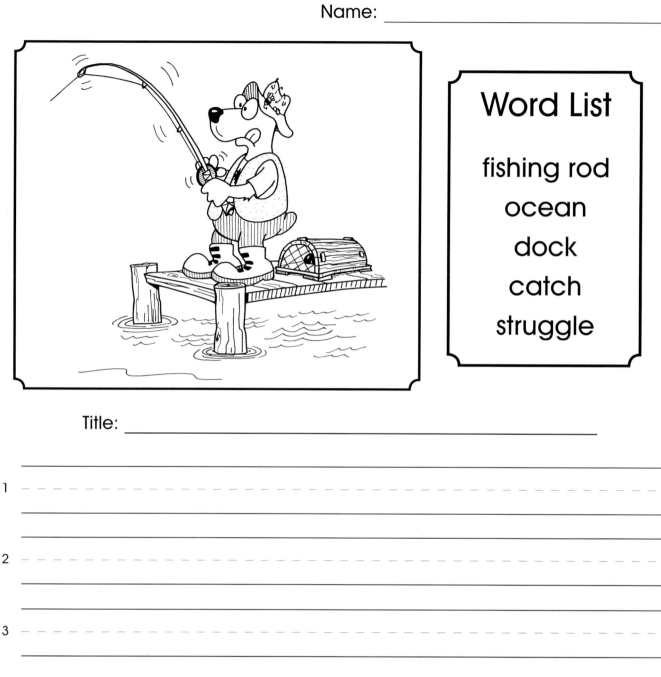

Word List

fishing rod

ocean

dock

catch

struggle

Title: _____

1 _____

_____

2 _____

_____

3 _____

_____

4 _____

_____

5 _____

_____

6 _____

Animal Stories - Illustration 53

Name: _____

Word List

groundhog

farmer

crop

eat

angry

Title: _____

1 _____

2 _____

3 _____

4 _____

5 _____

6 _____

Animal Stories - Illustration 54

Name: _____

Word List

slide

park

chicken

fast

climb

Title: _____

1 _____

2 _____

3 _____

4 _____

5 _____

6 _____

Animal Stories - Illustration 55

Name: _____

Word List

motorcycle

speed

tiny

mouse

helmet

Title: _____

1 _____

_____

2 _____

_____

3 _____

_____

4 _____

_____

5 _____

_____

6 _____

_____

Animal Stories - Illustration 56

Name: _____

Word List

jungle

leopard

swamp

parrot

wild

Title: _____

1 _____

_____

2 _____

_____

3 _____

_____

4 _____

_____

5 _____

_____

6 _____

_____

Animal Stories - Illustration 57

Name: _____

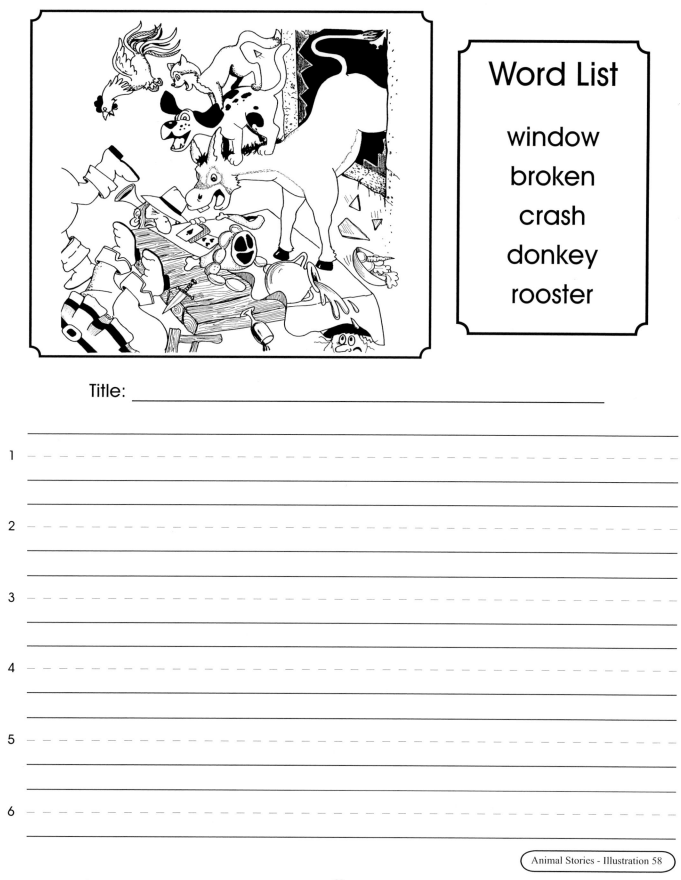

Word List

window

broken

crash

donkey

rooster

Title: _____

1 _____

2 _____

3 _____

4 _____

5 _____

6 _____

Animal Stories - Illustration 58

Story Starters

Name: _____ Title: _____

1 _____

2 _____

3 _____

4 _____

5 _____

6 _____

7 _____

8 _____

9 _____

10 _____